MANAGE YOUR LANGUAGE

How to Get Ahead in Health and Social Care

This is where the journey really starts

CAROLYN M HOLMES

First published in 2019
Imprint: Independently published

Thanks to Awais Qureshi, Hassaan Zakir Awan
And Atiq-ur-Rehman for the cover picture.

Printed edition ISBN: 9781710233872

The right of Carolyn M Holmes to be identified as the author of this work has been asserted in accordance with sections 77 and 78 of the Copyright, Designs and Patents Act 1988.

All rights reserved. No part of this book may be reproduced in any material form (including photocopying or storing in any medium by electronic means and whether or not transiently or incidentally to some other use of this publication) without the written permission of the copyright holders except in accordance with the provisions of the Copyright, Designs and Patents Act 1988. Applications for the copyright holders' written permission to reproduce any part of this publication should be addressed to the publishers.

Copyright 2019 Carolyn M Holmes

With special thanks to my family and friends;

you know who you are!

'If language is not correct, then what is said is not what is meant; if what is said is not what is meant, then what must be done remains undone; if this remains undone, morals and art will deteriorate; if justice goes astray, the people will stand about in helpless confusion. Hence there must be no arbitrariness in what is said. This matters above everything.'

Confucius, Chinese philosopher & reformer
(551 BC - 479 BC)

FOREWORD

This is a valuable and concise book. Coming from a long background in health, social care work, and education, Carolyn distils many years of learning and experience to demystify and expose the true meaning of the oft used phrases in these professional fields. Basing, what is in here, on what she has herself experienced in many meetings with managers and practitioners at different levels, Carolyn captures some key phrases and lessons.

For those of us who have been involved in such work for a long time the terms and phrases set out here are remarkably familiar. What the book does so well is to interpret them from an appreciation of the 'back story' and context of their use, allowing us to be able to respond appropriately and effectively in such situations, and indeed to make use of them when appropriate, to' impress' others!

Whilst substance, values and effective methods and supervision are the key bedrock of social work social care, health and the real basis of our work, this compact and focused book help us to navigate from an understanding of these discourses to be able to best understand the background to what is being said, and how to make use of this in the best way possible. This is all done in a light-hearted way which makes it easy to work through.

Some examples I enjoyed most from amongst of the phrases and the translations are:

'I'd like to share our adventure this is what good looks like'- translation: 'I'd like to tell you what a great manager I am and what a great job I've done'.

'We are on a learning curve; we are getting there' - translation: 'We are just working out what we should be doing what we are trying to figure it out'.

'The wheels are coming off the bus! We may need to grease the wheels' – translation: 'It's an emergency! Everything is going wrong to this project. We need help fast'.

In summary, this is a really useful book to gain a lot of knowledge in a short time, for all those involved in health and social care, and particularly for those who are learning the language maybe for the first time.

Professor Brian Littlechild, PhD

Research Lead for Social Work, University of Hertfordshire/Vice President, European Research Institute for Social Work

CONTENTS

Foreword v

Introduction 1

Chapter 1 Path to success. We are all on a journey 10

Chapter 2 Not again! This is a car crash waiting to happen. 27

Chapter 3 Bounce back. I need to download. Moving swiftly on! 41

Conclusion 57

Acknowledgements 60

INTRODUCTION

"She speaks our language rather than all that ivory tower stuff." ~ Carys Martin

"We are all saying the same thing in different words." ~ Hugh Prather

Manage your language: how to get on and get ahead in health and social care' is the first practical book with frequently used words and real-life phrases used by managers and staff in the health and social care sector in the UK. It provides light-hearted and cynical translations for you to make sense of what is or isn't being said. Do you want to be promoted and move up the pile? Then this book is for you. Using

INTRODUCTION

these words and speaking like a leader will give you an advantage, impress others and put you on the 'same page as them'. It can help you make your way up the slippery slope of the health and social care industry ladder, if that's what you want to do and confuse everyone in the process.

The book will also show, through suggested translations, that using complex language does not help get the job done. Instead, using simpler English could become the new 'normal' and make the world a better place where everyone understands each other and could get on with the job.

This a start at a guide, and as someone said, 'there are no definite, definitives.' What, they were trying to say there are no answers to everything! There's the old saying that "you don't know what you don't know." But how will you know when someone is trying to pull the wool over your eyes and mislead you intentionally or otherwise? We can all end up going 'down the rabbit hole,' if the language and meaning are lost. If we misunderstand even a little of what has been said, the conversation will go in the wrong direction and we forget what we were there for in the first place.

Often, we joke that it's quicker and easier for everyone to look at the simpler, shorter 'easy read' pictorial versions of key health and social care documents. So that says a lot. If we don't understand it and we work in health and social care, what must it be like for the public and those who are hoping to work in this area?

So, let's cut through the jargon — the 'corporate lingo' — so that we can communicate, communicate, communicate, and have a clear, consistent message. For some, health and social care is a 'monster' they don't understand. Managers like to be open, clear, and involve the public in consultations about changes to services. But from what I overheard recently, 'the health and social care system takes people on a very confusing journey.' It's as if we are expecting the public to be bilingual, to learn our language, in order to understand what we are saying. Many employees are aware of how complicated what they are trying to say is. 'It is far from easy to articulate, let alone deliver. I've just given you the idiot's guide to the toolkit.'

Most of us don't want the public or staff to switch off as soon as they hear something they don't understand and feel too silly to ask what it really means. As one manager commented, "We need to make sure the information is accessible, understandable, and sense-checked!" Many people want to contribute and take part in helping with new developments in health and social care in what is sometimes called coproduction or public participation. They can also find it helpful to learn the phrases too, but really shouldn't have to.

Language can be loaded with meaning, such as describing people as 'cases' or 'clients' who are having a 'review' or an 'assessment'. This can create feelings of exclusion and create an instant barrier in conversations, which are meant to help a situation but instead of making it worse. Now there are movements to break down these language barriers in social care. But it's a habit many of us have got into, which can be hard to break; but break it we must if we are to make change happen.

Managers across health and social care often complain that they need a common language to understand *each other*! Then they spend a lot of time trying to 'align language across pathways and programmes.' Where does this come from and what does it mean? One reason is that when we join any organisation or company, we learn to fit in, belong, be part of the culture and the way things are done there. Language is part of this, so keep using some of the key occupational words so that you can become accepted and appear knowledgeable quite quickly.

So in a way, we 'pass' words and phrases on like a virus, like Covid 19. This has certainly changed our vocabulary. Or is it that by using metaphors, speaking using pictures, we understand a situation better? Someone said, "We enjoyed the imagery; imagery speaks to

INTRODUCTION

us." So, there are some advantages to speaking in this way for some people; it helps them make sense of a complicated situation in which we often find ourselves.

But why is it that the more senior managers are often heard extensively using phrases in this book? Have they done well in their careers partly because they know what (or what not) to say and how to say it? Does it make them appear intelligent, knowing, and important? Does it buy them time since no one is sure what is being said or really going on but don't want to question their superiors? Is it because of their education? Is it to do with status, or is it just the culture, the way of doing things, which is expected when you work as a manager in health and social care? A friend said to me, 'Those people at the top love their jargon.' So, I'm not the only one who has noticed what's going on. Have you?

Certainly, some people have worked this to their advantage. "It helps when working with senior staff that you reword and explain something. You don't come over as 'pink and fluffy'; you talk about targets instead! I see language not as a barrier if you can jump over the hurdle." So here, the member of staff had worked out how to talk and what to say to senior managers in order to be heard, influence and do well.

Are they aware? Do they know when they use code or jargon? Some say, "Does that sound like gobbledygook? Are you with me?" "What do you think?" Another said, "EQSD," sounding like she knows what she is talking about! " Acronyms, which are shortened words abbreviated into capitals, can be found everywhere in health and social care. There are so many that employees can't remember often ask each other what they mean or even make them up! So that is a whole other book.

So does all this focus of language matter? Who does it matter to? Would people change if they know they were doing it? One person commented, "Most things go wrong because of communication, expectations,

INTRODUCTION

and language." Confucius, in the introductory quote of this book, reminds us of the ultimate consequences if we do not understand each other. What can be more serious than the delivery of high-quality healthcare by a motivated, included workforce who understand what is needed to deliver an efficient first-class service? Let's talk about what we want to happen. When are you free for a meeting? I think it would be good to put some time in the diary...

1

PATH TO SUCCESS

WE ARE ALL ON A JOURNEY

"A journey of a thousand miles begins with a single step." ~ Lao Tzu

"When life throws you a curveball, hit it out of the park" ~ Unknown

Talking about journeys, the distance left before we get to our destination, whether it's travelling or talking about how much extra work there is to do, is very common in health and social care. There is no doubt that you will hear this word almost every day. The journey represents the work not yet done but needs to be done, and the distance we have all covered whilst indirectly admitting that we still have not reached our goal due to lack of money, time, expertise, staff, etc. It is almost like an apology for not yet completing what we set out to do, but saying, "Hey, it's ok because there is so much to do. We are on a journey together, so it's ok after all. Rome wasn't built in a day."

When talking about your journey, here are some useful words to use:

Adventure, curve, curveball, direction, go, grail, journey, loop, manoeuvre, mapping, marathon, onboarding, paths, pathways, route, run, scoping, signposting, signs, step, track, trail, trailblazing, travels, tread, tunnel, walk, and way. **Here are real-life phrases with suggested translations about what is being said.**

Phrase	Suggested Translation
We are on an **adventure**; we are all very much on a journey.	Well, it did not work out as I said it would, but hey, we're all together in this mess.
I'd like to share our **adventure**; this is what good looks like.	I'd like to tell you what a great manager I am and what a great job I've done.
We are way behind the **curve** and not even on the **curve**!	We are way behind schedule and haven't even started!
We are on a learning **curve**; we are getting there.	Well, we are just working out what we should be doing, but we are trying to figure it out.
It's been a giant learning **curve**; let's keep talking.	Well, I didn't understand it at the beginning, and I sure don't now.

Just to throw a **curveball** into the mix….	Well, I've got something to tell you, which isn't good news…
We need to watch out for the **curveballs** and always have a plan. I know, so let's develop a plan.	I need you to be on the lookout for things going wrong all over the place and know how you are going to react. Thanks for your offer to work out a plan of what to do next.
Can you give me some **direction** please on what you want me to do next?	I'm unsure what the next steps I should be taking are from your initial instructions.
Have a **go** at weaving stories into your everyday work.	Just make it up as you go along; no change there.
We are **going** in the right direction. We are supporting the high-level direction of travel.	At last, we are on track and doing what the Board thinks it wants us to do.

We are **going** through a period of stability, so let's crack on.	Let's get on with it; nothing has gone wrong for a while.
We are **going** there tomorrow. Didn't I send you an invite?	Didn't you check your inbox or were you not important enough to have been invited? I'll email it to you.
Discussions are ongoing; we need to keep the interest **going**.	They are still talking about it. Everyone's fed up with it. We can't let them forget what an important project we are working on.
In my personal experience, if we are **going** to do anything, it should be this…	I think, given my seniority, that you should listen to my advice.
We are **going** off-piste!	We are going horribly wrong! Help!
May I ask where have we **got to** on this? The others feel they are out of the	Can you give me an update please on the project? Other team members feel like they

loop and they don't know what's going on.	do not know the latest information on what's happening.
We would like to have a register; that is the holy **grail!**	Well, we've been talking about developing this for some time now, and it's still our number one priority.
The whole way we are travelling is a long **journey**. How will the journey change in the future?	Well, it's going to be at least 5 years before anything changes and then it will all change again, so let's just keep talking about the journey.
I hope everyone is excited about the **journey**; it's going to be an exciting journey!	Let's hope you feel as pleased with yourself as I do about my great ideas about what we are doing next.

We are barrelling along; I would love to bottle that **journey**.	We are going faster than I would like, but I want to remember the great things I've done so I can remind you all later.
It's not a race but a **journey**.	What I really mean is that it's a race, so hurry up!
So where are we on the **journey**?	I'm not sure where we are with this, but I'll give you a general idea. Any suggestions before I start?
On this **journey** of improvement, how will we really know we are making a difference?	We wanted to get better and know it will take a long time, but how will we know that the money we've spent on this will make an impact?
It's been a challenging but exciting **journey**, and we are all learning from each other.	This experience has been a bit of a roller coaster ride for me, but thankfully, you have got me out of the shit.

We are not at the end of the **journey** yet by any stretch of the imagination.	Oh dear, there's so much left to do.
I have really loved watching their **journey** over the last three years.	It's been wonderful following their progress over the last three years, thanks to my support.
Clearly, the email has had a rather confusing **journey** around the system!	Well, I'm sorry you didn't get the email sooner. We must have sent it to the wrong people by mistake or forgotten you.
The health and social care system takes people on a very confusing **journey.**	We do our best so that people don't understand what we are doing.
Keep the faith! The **journey** you are on may take longer than you expected.	Keep going; we have plenty of time. Don't worry about this journey; the next one is around the corner!

They will get together via Skype to present their individual **journeys.**	If they can get the computers working, they will each tell everyone what they think they want to hear.
We are in the **loop**; we are in the **loop**!	At last, they have included us in their meetings, so we can find out what's going on.
We haven't any room for **manoeuvre**. We need to report back on the milestones on a monthly basis.	I can't do anything about it. They want to know if we are meeting the target every month. Help!
When the exec team come on board, there should be some **mapping** opportunities.	Don't get too excited about some new work; it could take a while for the top team to decide.
So well done, everybody! Don't forget that this is a **marathon** and not a sprint.	I am so pleased with you all. But we are in this for the longer term, not just the short term. We need to keep going.

Has anyone got any questions about induction and **onboarding**?	Please don't ask me because I probably won't be able to answer your questions.
Our **paths** may cross in due course, with everything coming together.	Hopefully, I won't see you again anytime soon now that you've sorted my mess out for me.
All our **pathways** are the same!	Thank goodness we are approaching everything in the same way! Phew!
We need to have **routes** in. We need a **route** of escalation.	Who has contacts who can help us?
I've done a lot of **scoping**; I've done the modelling and identified what we need to do.	Well, I've been incredibly busy lately. I've done what needs to be done in this project, created a few different examples of what could

	happen and then created an action plan.
Signposting is a banned word; we should say 'connecting'!	One day we will be saying 'signposting' again.
We need the support. The **signs** are good that we will get it!	Oh dear, things are not going well, but I've said we need more money and from my high-level discussions, I believe it's coming.
Whoa, whoa, whoa! We need to take a **step** back; I don't have a clue what you're talking about!	Hold on a minute! Can we just go over what you just said? I really don't understand it.
You are going to have to take a **step** back.	Trust me, you need to keep out of this for now while I get to know senior management.

MANAGE YOUR LANGUAGE

She's just **stepped** out of the office for a little bit. You have just missed her; she's not at her desk at the moment.	You're too late. She doesn't really want to speak to you. Send an email, which she will then ignore as usual.
We must not take **steps** that don't add any value.	Let's just get rid of all the waffle that means everything.
We are not **stepping** out of the picture without rigorous enforcement interoperability and the ability to swap out aspects.	I'm not leaving, until I get everyone to do what I want, that is if they can understand me!
This guy has a bit of a **track** record.	He's well-known around here, so be careful.
They are off **track** and not planning to deliver by the end of the year. Where are we? Are we on track? In	The other team are behind and will not achieve the plan they announced earlier this year. But what about us? Are we ok? Can we

hindsight, we need an audit trail.	prove it? Check the emails for the evidence!
Onwards and upwards! We are back on **track** to deliver after a slow start!	Yes! I'm doing a great job in leading you to success. It's working beautifully.
Let's **track** the data. We may need to make changes to get the right traction.	Keep an eye on the budget. I may have to ask for more money again.
We need to follow the email **trail**.	Just keep everything in writing and don't lose it. We need to cover our tracks.
We secured it; we are **trailblazing**!	Yes, we got the funding. We are leading from the front as usual.
If you come across it in your **travels.**	If you can look for what I've lost, please do, since I can't remember what I did with it. If not no worries.

This is an important opportunity for stakeholders to engage with us. However, we need to **tread** reasonably carefully; it's fragile.	This is a key meeting with everyone, but we better play safe. It could all go terribly wrong.
We have **tunnel** vision.	Can you see what I see?
Rather than rushing in, I suggest we take a **walk** and see?	Well, my way is the best...
We need to be upfront, honest, transparent, constructive, and sensible about this. But he's not **walking** the talk.	There's a real problem with us being clear about what's really going on, but he's not helping because he's not doing what he said he will do. What shall we do?

The golden thread should run all the **way** through.	What is the most important idea in this project? I'm not sure what that is right now, but I'm sounding like I do. It should be seen in everything that we do.
We will need to articulate how this approach can be embedded into the **way** we do things, in our everyday work, into the fabric of the organisation.	Can you get Comms on board to write a simple paragraph so that people understand what we are doing for a change?
Well, if that's the **way** we are going…	Well, if that's what you want to do, but I don't agree with you.
Our personas get in our **way**!	Yes, we know that we think we are great, but hey, we know our weaknesses, so let's move on.
It's definitely a two-**way** process.	I need to hear your ideas so I can use them as my own.

I'll arrange a four-**way** conversation.	I'll arrange a teleconference for the four of us when I can get around to organising one. Let's hope everyone turns up this time.

2

NOT AGAIN!

THIS IS A CAR CRASH WAITING TO HAPPEN

"The ship is sinking. We must try and save it. Help me get it into the lifeboat." ~ Spike Milligan

"We are in danger of setting up travel agents who don't have any holidays!" ~ Unknown

We have much to thank the world of transport for in helping us on our way in health and social care, from the millions of journeys we and our patients make to and from hospitals, offices, GP (doctors) surgeries. From cars to buses to boats and trains, there's so much to talk about! The visual nature of our transport system, especially when things go wrong, adds to our wish to emphasise, and dramatize what we are saying, just in case the person we were talking to wasn't listening, had nodded off, or was on the phone. You get what I mean?

When talking about transport, here are some useful words to use:

Accelerate, board, boat, bridge, bus, car crash, deck, driven, driver, keel, liner, motoring, navigating, park, passported, pedal, rails, reverse, road, roadmap, Skoda/Rolls Royce, speed, steer, traction, traffic, train, travel, and wheel. **Here are real-life phrases, with suggested translations, about what is being said.**

Phrase	Suggested translation
Just a quick question… Will this **accelerate** the **delivery** of planned projects?	If you don't mind me asking, will your idea make any difference to our progress or is it just one of your fantasies?
I am **accelerating**, and I am starting to see a shift!	I'm getting better and faster at this and now the results are coming in even though I didn't understand what you wanted me to do in the first place. But does that matter?
You can take your foot off the **accelerator** once you have mitigated the risk.	I don't mean that really. Just keep going; there is always a risk, but hey, it's fun!
We are fortunate that we have our new colleagues on **board.**	Thank goodness they have started. There is so much work we can give them to get on with.

This is a fruitless task. Are you still on **board**?	It's a complete waste of time, I know, but I still need your help.
We must stay on **board** even when we want to get rid of the oars and jump ship.	I wish I could get out of here like you, but I still have a mortgage and bills to pay.
I was a **boat** rocker today.	I upset everyone today. I told them what I thought, and it was great!
We are seeing ourselves as the **bridge** to community assets.	We are so important! How would they manage without us?
It's the 'hit by a **bus**' theory! It's like no one tested it!	They think they can do anything today since they might get run over and die tomorrow. Didn't they think of checking that it would work properly and withstand the pressure?

We are hopping on and off the **bus**!	Can you just make your minds up? Don't ask me. By the way, I haven't got a clue!
The wheels are coming off the **bus**! We may need to grease the wheels.	It's an emergency! Everything is going wrong with this project. We need help fast.
I'm sorry I threw you under the **bus** the other day.	I'm not really sorry. I was protecting myself; I need to look after number one, you know!
The penny is dropping. It is a **car crash**!	I've only just realised; this is a disaster!
It's top secret! This is a **car crash** waiting to happen... What we know is coming onto the horizon.	I've used my crystal ball and I know this is going belly up. Just keep it between us for now.

Crisis management usually indicates all hands-on **deck.**	When things are bad, we need to move everyone from what they should be doing to sort the mess out.
It's going to be locally **driven**. It's just going to be learning all the way.	Well, they have developed the responsibility down to us, so we shall make it up together.
Given that there is a big system **driver** and we know there is a big emphasis on this locally/regionally/nationally.	I have no idea what I'm talking about, but it sounds good.
We need leaders and **drivers**.	Look no further. I am here!
Who is in the **driving** seat?	Who is in charge here? Take me to your leader!
We are **driving** forward from the centre, so let's pick up the pace.	We are leading this programme from within, so

	let's get on with it and go faster.
We need to get back on an even **keel.**	Let's get back to business as usual, whatever usual is.
There is no blame culture around here. We try and get people on an even **keel**. When we talk about risk, we can't just carry it around in our heads.	Oh yes, there is a blame culture. It's just that we are not telling anyone. We need to know where things are going wrong for when we plan the next restructure.
That is not going to shift the system; it's not going to turn the **liner**!	No matter what you think, it's just not going to work; the problem is just too big.
Can we get **motoring** on that quote?	Let's get a move on. We need the money now.
We are **motoring** along with the programme.	Yes, what a great team. We were praised at the board for our success.

The problem on the ground is that **navigating** through systems is difficult.	What we are finding is that trying to find out who does what around here is taking a long time.
We need to **park** this issue for a minute, put it in the too-difficult pile and come back to it later.	Let's just put your comment aside until later when we will all have forgotten about it. It's just not relevant, so let's talk more about what I think is important.
So often we go down the road of eligibility and people get **passported.**	Our criteria are not worth the paper they are written on…
My foot is firmly on the **pedal**.	I'm getting on with it. Let me reassure you when I'm not having a coffee.

The other team are behind and gone off the **rails**. Are we ok?	Have you heard the news? We're doing well because the other team are in trouble!
There is an alternative option. We need to be thinking of **reverse** incentives.	We must consider how we can get people to do things we want, without them realising.
We've had some bumps in the **road**, but we are learning as we go.	It's been a bit difficult at times, and we have made some mistakes, but that's just part of the experience.
There are a lot of bumps on the **road**. We do thrive on a bump in the **road**. Those bumps are a seed; they help us to make something work!	Lots of things go wrong all the time, but we do love a challenge and telling everyone about our lessons learned.

We are working on a digital **roadmap**.	For the past few years, we have been talking about sharing records across health and social care. We are still talking about it and talking about it...
It does what it says on the tin! Why have a **Rolls Royce** when a Skoda will do?	We know what to expect. We are on an efficiency drive. Why pay more for something that is perfectly good and a lot cheaper?
We see it as a **Rolls Royce** service.	What we do is simply great! Just don't ask me if we've had any complaints. I don't know!
Systems change at the **speed** of the slowest person.	There is always one person slowing everything down and we need to find that person fast if we are going to make any change. It's good.

Can you give me a **steer** on the submission because they got a push back?	Can you tell me what they said about our paper? I won't tell anyone else! I hear they said it was rubbish…
Is there a **steer** around the accountability?	Does anyone know who is taking responsibility for this mess?
Frankly, at the moment, a lot of what needs to get done isn't getting done. We need some more **traction** on this.	I really despair what's been going on here; it's just a disaster. We need to make some progress or I'll be in trouble!
We are hoping to get some **traction** over the **delivery** plan.	We are expecting that, if all goes well, we will make some progress on making things happen on time.
These things work better when they are driven by staff and supported by the	Well, we have learned the hard way that when we ignore the staff or lie to them, they tend to leave.

organisation to gain **traction.**	
I've seen some email **traffic**, so I just escalated it.	There have been lots of emails. I can't be bothered to read them, so I've just forwarded them to the managers who have more time to read them.
Yes, I am pulling together all the work. It's all in **train**.	What I will do when I have a moment is to look at my very long to-do list and try and remember what you asked me to do.
We are in danger of setting up **travel** agents who don't have any holidays!	That sounded good, didn't it? What I mean is that we are pushing the ball down the road, giving responsibility for delivering services to other groups whom we have decided not to fund.
Are we linked to their approach? We need to save	Did you get a look at their plans? I want to know what

| ourselves from reinventing the **wheel**. | they are doing, so we don't look like we are useless. |

3

BOUNCE BACK

I NEED TO DOWNLOAD! MOVING SWIFTLY ON...

"Remember that if plan A fails, you have 25 letters left." ~ Anonymous

"Reverse is sometimes the best way forward."
~ Oliver Burkeman

At work, we are always moving, either tapping our feet, getting a cup of tea, helping a patient, a colleague, or a manager. We are sending emails, making telephone calls, attending meetings, providing care and support, but how do we do this? The answer is: in many ways! Read on....and start using some different words to explain your style!

When talking about moving, here are some useful words to use:

Bedding, bounce, branched, breakthrough, bring, cascade, catch, caught up, come, churn, connect, crossover, delivery, down, download, drop, dynamic, evolve, falling, floating, forward, grow, impact, inflate, jog, jump, leap, leave, lift, linking, momentum, move, movement, nip, offload, pick, ping, pop, progress, push, putting, run, shifted, splash, stalling, start, stretch, take, throw, tick, transition, turned, upend, upwards, whipped, and wrap.

Phrase	Suggested Translation
The next 3 weeks are **bedding** down and getting on with it.	We haven't planned for the next 3 weeks, but it will give us time to work out what we really need to do and then we can get started.
Do we need to **bounce** this back?	I'm not sure what to do. Are you? Let's send it back to them.
People are **bouncing** around health and social care services.	Do you know where the patients are? Yes, we sent them over there to see you. Please send them back when you have finished.
We **branched** out to see if there were wider people to involve.	I've sent the information to some of my friends. They've helped me out before.
I've had a **breakthrough** in the past couple of days!	Eureka! At last, I've worked out better late than never.

There is a ray of sunshine. **Bringing** people on the bus with you helps **bring** joy at work!	Well, if you can persuade enough people to look at things your way, you have done a great job that day.
We will **cascade** this via email.	We will send this information to as many people we can think of in the hope that somebody will find it interesting.
We need to put some time in to have a bit of a **catch-up**.	I haven't seen you for ages. Let's meet for lunch for good gossip.
We are **catching** people falling through the net!	There are a lot of holes in the nets, so that's why there are a lot of people falling through them
Come and join the party! The best is yet to **come**!	We're having such a great time here. Come and meet our team. We're having a fab time. There is no stopping us now.

MANAGE YOUR LANGUAGE

Unless anyone else would want to **come** in?	Can anyone fit a word in edgeways or should I carry on talking?
I'll **come** back with a form of words.	I'll quickly write something on the back of an envelope and come back to you when I'm ready.
It will be very interesting to see what comes out of it. Do **come** back to me if you need to.	Come back to me with all the gossip. Tell me what they're doing, please. Don't be shy.
This is an opportunity to shape the things to **come**.	Can you listen to me? I need to persuade you somehow; I've got a great idea!
Is the money **coming** down?	Which pot of money are we going to use now? Have you spoken to the powers that be about our predicament?
It's stinky and smelly, needs to go in the washing	Right now, everything is going wrong, but trust, me I am

45

machine and will **come** out all fresh for the line!	your leader. It will all be alright in the end!
The consultants are **coming** to do some change management.	They are paying a lot of money for people to come in and tell us what we already know. Do they ever learn?
There is a lot of **churn** here.	People keep leaving and I don't know why.
The problem is that it gets lost in the day-to-day **churn**.	The issue is that we have so many important things to do that we don't know what to do first. The most important things are lost, so we can't see the wood for the trees!
We need to **connect** the system with itself!	Do you understand what I'm talking about? I don't! What I mean is, nobody is talking to each other across all the different organisations.
It went **down** like a cup of cold sick!	Well, they didn't like that one. I can tell you that for nothing!

I need to **download**. Moving swiftly on…	I am so frustrated I want to scream! Anyway, what were you saying?
Everything is ticking along nicely. We have used the very best evidence base and we are getting the model pinned **down**.	We have stolen everybody else's good ideas and passed them off as our own, so we are getting on marvellously!
Do you want to **drop** her?	Well, do you want to just leave her out of the meetings going forward?
I'll **drop** her an email. Do you want to **drop** her number down?	Why am I asking for her number when I'm going to send her an email?
We all need to pick up and **drop**!	To get on, you just need to start one thing and then switch to something else whenever your manager says.

The interesting **dynamic** in this is that we need to go where the energy is.	In a nutshell, we've just got to get on with it.
The document will continue to **evolve.**	I've just said that for effect. I haven't finished it really and I've moved on to something else far more interesting.
Patients are **falling** through the cracks.	Have you seen the patients? Where are they?
I'm like the duck **floating** on top of the bathwater at the moment. Not a lot is going to happen!	I had a bit too much to drink last night, so don't expect me to do a lot today.
Are you happy to take that action going **forward**?	Do me a favour and help me out even though you are busy.
I totally agree with you. You need to go **forward** and don't look back.	Yes, you're right. Never look back at your mistakes.

MANAGE YOUR LANGUAGE

This morning, we will spend the time looking **forward**, using our crystal ball! What are we trying to do here?	Today, we will make things up as we go along. If someone could remind me what we're here to talk about in the first place that would be a good start
Looking **forward,** this is going to be essential going in the future.	I need to show I know what's happening next. Tell me your ideas so I can impress the board when I make my impression.
The mental health agenda continues to burgeon and **grow** large.	I like complicated words.
We need to **grow** our tribe!	Let's find people who look like us, speak like us, and agree with everything we say.
These measures will have an i**mpact** on demand. Are we in danger of artificially i**nflating** the numbers?	Can you change the data?

49

Ooh... **jog** my memory, please!	I can't remember the ins and outs of this. Help!
Can I **jump** in to support you there?	I like you so much I'm just going to agree with everything you say.
They were **jumping** far into the future.	We just get through each day as it happens. How can they think about what could happen next year?
We are **jumping** hurdles!	Why do they make it so difficult for us all the time? Are they trying to catch us out?
As soon as everyone **jumped** on the same page, everything came together.	When they came around to what I was thinking, it was fantastic!
We **leapt** into recruitment!	Not really! It's taken us 6 months to get going on this one.

I must **leave** now. Sorry to love you and **leave** you.	The traffic's terrible. I better leave so I can get home on time for lunch.
I will **lift** the information and put it in the report.	Who's done the work before? I'll copy it immediately. I don't have many original thoughts of my own.
With algorithms increasingly taking over the clinical **lifting** in the NHS....	Thank God I'm not in charge of finance anymore. I never could get my head around Excel spreadsheets.
We will be **linking** up with you in the South East.	Yes, we will be making some strategic relationships across the country.
I've done a bit of a think piece on how this all **links**	I have written a few words on an email and called a think piece.

together and would be grateful for your views.	
We do an initial call-out at the beginning of the programme in order to claim **momentum**.	Send email to the usual suspects just to prove we've done something.
How are you going to **move** your metric?	How are you going to make the figures add up?
We are creating a social **movement**. You know, it's only a **movement** if it moves without you!	This is a cheap way of getting things done on a big scale, especially if you just let it go.
I'll **nip** upstairs. See you in a bit. I need to **offload.**	I really need to talk to someone. I'll just pop upstairs. I'll be back in a little while.
I just wish they would **pick** up the phone and call instead of sending emails.	They just rely on an email trail and will not pick up the phone to talk to me, which does not help at all.
I'll **ping** you an email. Can you just ping it to me?	Let's play email ping pong.

Could you **pop** and see her?	Be a dear and go see her.
Like anything, it is all a work in **progress**. We need to flesh out the **progress** and move further. Let's take the plunge and take it forward.	As usual, it's taking far too long. You need to add some detail to the plan and get on with it. People are asking questions.
They did **push** through. It's a testament to the calibre of their professionalism and enthusiasm.	It's just amazing what they did in the face of such difficulty day in, day out.
Can you **push** back?	Just say no!
But he's not **putting** out the fires over here!	What's he doing over there? Why is he bothering them with helping them sort their mess out? He needs to come here!

They don't have someone to **run** with it. Can you give them a hand, please?	They don't have enough staff. Everybody has left. I said you would help them out.
I've just realised I said up and **running** several times in the conversation!	Oh dear, I just keep repeating myself. How embarrassing.
We also received significant feedback that we are **running** out of time.	I've had a ********** from the boss. You need to get on with it for a change!
They are **running** to his tune, rather than standing up to him!	Here we go again…
Don't be afraid to **splash** someone or fail!	You can fail if you want to. Then it will just make me look better.
This is not **stalling**; it is intelligence gathering!	What do you mean I haven't done anything?
And finally, this slide gives a picture of the journey of what needs to happen. This	At last, we have got around to telling everyone about what we think we are going

is where the journey is really going to **start**.	to do as of today or sometime not soon.
It's been a slow **start**. It has been a difficult journey, so we are at different stages of the journey.	This has been like pulling teeth and it has taken far too long.
Stretch assignments provide an opportunity for skills and knowledge exposure in a different area of work.	We have some projects with unrealistic deadlines if you would like a challenge.
We will **take** that conversation forward tomorrow.	Thank you. I'll conveniently forget this conversation.
It's all very well, but I'm just **throwing** it out there!	Feel free to ignore what I say at your peril.
We are box-**ticking**; but it is a box to be ticked!	We have 20 boxes; how many do you have?
It's going to take time. We are in **transition**. We haven't really **shifted** from the 80s, 90s model!	Nothing really changes around here. We just recycle the same ideas every 10-20 years.

The most frustrating thing is that she wants it **turned** around quickly.	I'm going on holiday next week and my manager is onto me to finish it now, but I have my last-minute shopping to do.
We can't do something different; it will **upend** the contract. It's all very fragile!	Don't ask me to change anything. Let's put it on the too-difficult pile.
We need to manage **upward**s, downwards, inside, and outside!	Whatever way you look at it, we are all doing everybody else's jobs; it's duplication all over the place.
Who **whipped** my chair?	Who's sitting in my chair?
The organisation needs to **wrap** around that frame and then reframe again.	Don't worry, we need to accept the plan that has been imposed on us and then readjust to what suits us best.

CONCLUSION

"Boy, those French. They have a different word for everything." ~ Steve Martin

"Every day is a school day!" ~ Unknown

In health and social care, we have the inherent tendency to want to fix things, make them better and move on swiftly to the next crisis. So, what can we do about this situation regarding the use of jargon and nonsensical phrases in health and social care? Some people say at the beginning of a meeting, "If anyone uses abbreviations or words that don't make sense, please ask me to explain it!" It takes a special person (I can name only one) who makes sure that everyone understands what is being said once a meeting or presentation has started. But surely, we shouldn't have to be

CONCLUSION

decoding the language we hear. But if we did explain every word that isn't clear, would we ever finish the presentation?

There are new phrases popping up all the time, so we just keep on learning and laughing! As they say, 'Asset-based approaches are the new buzzword.' We all have a different understanding of what on earth is going on, or not going on, depending on our experience and background. So, let's all learn from each other too! Don't worry; just learn as you go along. As someone said recently, "It's not just one step; you may take a few steps back. But if you take the steps in the right order, you will get there in the end." Another commented, "We are trying to make sense of it now! The best is yet to come!" And I suspect they are right!

We have this ability as professionals to make things extremely complicated. We need to start to think about how we can be active participants in managing our language and the way we speak. We need to 're-write the rule book', win hearts and minds, persuade others and change cultures. It's not easy to simplify and make sense of what we call a 'complex landscape.' Don't give up. Keep the faith and keep on pushing for a new way of communicating.

How are you loving the language? Are you starting to have any light bulb moments and thought, 'Aha! So that's what was going on?' Thank you for reading this book. Please recycle it and share it with your friends. I'd love to hear from you about your ideas and experiences of the language used in health and social care.

So, are you ready? The pain is certainly worth the gain. Let's start putting this into practice. As they say, "Every day is a school day!" If we all work together, we can make this happen, but I don't know where we will end up!

ACKNOWLEDGEMENTS

I would like to thank those who have supported and believed in me to make this book possible. Particularly my cat, Jess, who sits with me every day.

Thank you to my family, in particular my mother, the poet, Sheila Sanderson, who has passed her love of language onto me and my friend Liza Karle, with whom I compare our mutual writing progress. My appreciation goes to Awais, Hassan and Atiq for the cover design, as well as Professor Brian Littlechild, for his kind words in the forward to this book. Finally, I would like to thank Dr Susan England from Burnt Toast Editorial, for her kindness and no messing approach in working with me.

'Manage your language: how to get ahead in health and social care' builds on Carolyn's lifetime of work in supporting people in health and social care to do a good job. It shows her fascination with the spoken word and jargon and the popular phrases used by managers and staff in health and social care in the UK.

Carolyn started collecting words and phrases when she 'jumped over the fence' from working in social care for 30 years to work in the National Health Service, the publicly funded UK health service, as a health education manager. She thought she had landed in a different world and needed a translator! It's like something out of *The Office*! Unsurprisingly, she was not the only one who felt this way. As one manager commented, "There is so much bla bla bla. We need to be simple and jargon-free!" But it's not just in health care;

staff in social care complain about the language they use too!

If you enjoyed this book please look at the website www.manageyourlanguage.com or on Amazon, for the next book in the series, 'Absolutely I am the right person for you.'

Printed in Great Britain
by Amazon